МИНИСТЕРСТВО КУЛЬТУРЫ СССР

долгоиграющая

33
ОБОРОТА В МИНУТУ

АПРЕЛЕВСКИЙ ЗАВОД

ТУ—I кл.

Б
Д—2166

М. РАВЕЛЬ. ТРИО
ля минор
3 часть—Пассакалия
4 часть—Финал
Л. Н. ОБОРИН (ф-но)
Д. Ф. ОЙСТРАХ (скр.)
С. Н. КНУШЕВИЦКИЙ
(виолончель)

МИНИСТЕРСТВО КУЛЬТУРЫ СССР
ССCP
АПРЕЛЕВСКИЙ ЗАВОД

ДОЛГОИГРАЮЩАЯ

МИНИСТЕРСТВО КУЛЬТУРЫ СССР

Долгоиграющая

33
ОБОРОТА В МИНУТУ

АПРЕЛЕВСКИЙ ЗАВОД

ТУ—I кл.

B
Д—2165

М. РАВЕЛЬ, ТРИО
ля минор
1 часть—Модерато
2 часть—Скерцо
Л. Н. ОБОРИН (ф-но)
Д. Ф. ОЙСТРАХ (скр.)
С. Н. КНУШЕВИЦКИЙ
(виолончель)

ПРАВИЛА ПОЛЬЗОВАНИЯ ДОЛГОИГРАЮЩЕЙ ПЛАСТИНКОЙ

1. Долгоиграющая пластинка отличается от обычной пластинки большей длительностью звучания (в три-четыре раза).

2. Долгоиграющая пластинка предназначена для проигрывания на электропроигрывателе легким звукоснимателем со специальной иглой (корундовой или равноценной).

3. Проигрывание долгоиграющей пластинки на граммофоне не допускается.

4. Каждую пластинку следует хранить в отдельном конверте, в вертикальном положении, перед проигрыванием протирать пластинку фланелью.

5. Скорость вращения диска устанавливать согласно надписи на этикетке пластинки (78 или 33 обор. в минуту).

6. Не запускать и не останавливать диск при опущенном на пластинку звукоснимателе.

7. Опускать на пластинку и поднимать с нее звукосниматель плавно, без толчка.

PER ASPERA AD ASTRA

PER ASPERA AD ASTRA

THROUGH THE THORNS TO THE STARS

NATASHA HULL

SEAGULL PUBLISHING HOUSE
LONDON

Published in Great Britain in 2004 by
Seagull Publishing House Limited
14 Caterham Road London SE13 5AR

A catalogue record for this book
is available from the British Library.

ISBN 0-9543368-1-X

Editor: Ed Ewing
Design: PriceWatkins Design
Digital restoration: Natasha Vassilieva
Printed in Great Britain by
Cambridge University Press

CONTENTS

To Janet, who made me feel at home,
and Ray, my first listener.
Thanks!

NATASHA HULL, better known in Russia as Natasha Vassilieva, has been a legendary figure in rock culture since the early 1970s. Natasha's career as a rock photographer began with impromptu photo-sessions when her friends Boris Grebenshchikov and Seva Gakkel, members of the cult group Aquarium, performed their songs in her kitchen. Natasha began documenting concerts and tours by Leningrad's musicians, creating images of people, events and places that have since acquired a near-mythological status. In 1977 she co-founded *Roksi*, the Soviet Union's first samizdat journal devoted to rock culture, illustrated with her photographs. Her images provide a rare contemporary insight into the way in which rock, though without official sanction, was able to exist and be meaningful in Soviet society.

As Natasha's memoir suggests, rock played a unique role in the life stories of those who grew up in the Soviet Union. Inspired by snatches of rock and roll heard in poor quality on the BBC or Voice of America, young men got hold of guitars – sometimes with great difficulty – and founded rock groups. In the 1970s the rock scene functioned through personal connections, whether these were forged by sharing a passion for Western rock or speculating in smuggled Western LPs. Above all, rock and roll represented a lifestyle choice. Musicians went through the motions in low-paid day jobs, conserving their energies for concerts in friends' apartments and recordings made in amateur studios onto reel-to-reel tape. Concerts were advertised by word of mouth, albums distributed by fans making their own copies. Bands went on unofficial tours, gaining followers in the process. Awareness of the existence of home-grown, Russophone rock spread from its origins in closely connected circles. It became a phenomenon first at local level in Soviet cities, gradually encroaching into public culture nationwide, as its fans became too numerous to be ignored, filling large concert venues and gathering for open air festivals.

Music by Leningrad bands such as Aquarium and Zoopark, and later Kino and Alisa, contains different reactions to Soviet reality. Of particular importance in terms of arrangements, instrumentation and lyrical content are the obstacles faced by Soviet rock. Shortages of instruments and equipment, poor sound quality, concerts cancelled at the last minute by the authorities, criticism in the press, the near-impossible task of balancing secrecy and growing celebrity – all are reflected and thematised. Aquarium's 'Aristocrat', an individual's manifesto for avoiding strife by sitting on the roof smoking marijuana, contrasts with songs seeking to mobilise collective social discontent, epitomized by 'We're Together' by Alisa or Kino's 'Change'. Music from this era has out-lived its original associations, be they with dropping out of Soviet society or the camaraderie in adversity of being part of an officially unsanctioned culture. The Soviet incarnation of rock shaped its development in post-Soviet Russia. Self-conscious dilettantism, willingness to experiment, the importance of humour – all can be traced from the music of the 1970s to the present day.

Words and music were, of course, vital in rock culture; yet as with any movement in popular music in the West, Soviet rock had an important visual element. Musicians on the Leningrad scene sought to look like and present themselves as rock stars. Their fans, too, displayed their allegiances in their outward appearance. In the Soviet Union of the 1970s and 1980s this kind of overt display of an alternative that was not supposed to exist was highly provocative. Natasha's photographs did not merely document this culture, but fed back into it, as her prints were bought by fans and widely disseminated. They made the musicians' desired alternatives to everyday life seem *real*.

Natasha's photographs testify to the places in which rock musicians found themselves able to perform – private apartments, Soviet 'Houses of Culture', the stage of the theatre on Ulitsa Rubenshtein that became the Leningrad Rock Club. They also convey a sense of the paradoxical identity of the Soviet rock musician, simultaneously existing as a non-professional and as a star, struggling to survive in the face of official disapproval and scant material reward, yet evidently enjoying himself enormously. Perhaps most importantly, her images evoke this sense of fun, which is lacking in many other accounts of Soviet unofficial culture. The author of these photographs knows her subjects intimately, admires their style and daring, and passionately defends the way they – and she – have chosen to live.

Polly McMichael
Cambridge University

THE IDEA OF THIS BOOK was born during my exhibition in London in June 2003, thanks to numerous people asking numerous questions about our lives in Soviet Russia before Perestroika. My visitors seemed to be really interested, and generally knew precious little about this extraordinary time. For most people in the West Perestroika literally happened overnight. The crash of Communism was totally unexpected, the change of the political regime in that unimaginably huge part of the planet which lies to the east – from Poland to the Pacific – was a complete surprise. No explanations were given – it just happened.

So here I am with my version of the answers to the big questions about the end of Communism in Russia: Why and How?

For those of us there it was a long (for some lifelong) process of not only surviving the stupidity, cruelty and greed of the Communist regime, but actually living our lives ignoring the whole business.

Rock music was forbidden in the 70s and the beginning of the 80s. The Rolling Stones, Black Sabbath, Led Zeppelin and the rest were on the KGB's list of albums banned from entering the territory of the USSR. Sex, drugs and rock 'n' roll were evil Western ideas, and we couldn't possibly have those (officially, at least!) – we were supposed to be busy building a shining Communist Future.

Instead, it was merchant sailors who smuggled the first Beatles vinyl albums through the ports of the Soviet Empire, carrying them through in their laundry bags.

And that was how it started for my generation – with 'Ob-la-di, Ob-la-da' sounding ever more loudly on our side of the Curtain, which was becoming thinner and thinner with every new Beatles or Rolling Stones single.

Everybody knows that in the West rock was a rebellion against the establishment. Well, the same applies to Russia – the only difference being that it was the Communist regime that was the establishment there. And although in Russia rock started later and was originally heavily influenced by the West, it carried the same message of freedom and liberation. Obviously, being a rotten Western invention it was forbidden – never in history have the seeds of a forbidden fruit found more grateful soil. Soviet teenagers, suffocating in the grey concrete cell of Communist doctrine, were probably the best audience in the world. It was like an explosion – absolutely uncontrollable. One day, a tape-recorder as a weapon of mass destruction of ideology will find its place in the Moscow Museum of Revolution!

Let me say thank you to all citizens of the West who encouraged me with their curiosity, interest and attention, and to all who helped this project become a reality. But most of all, I want to say thank you to my daughter, whose love and trust were the only things which not only kept me going but sometimes actually kept me alive through all those years of absurd struggle on the verge of starvation and imprisonment. She was the first who ever raised her voice to defend me when two policemen arrested me and took me out of a venue with my hands behind my back. She said: "Let my mum go! She's not a criminal!" She was eight or maybe nine-years-old. At home we were listening to the same music. And this music was Rock.

Natasha Hull
London, 2004

9

THE BEGINNING
LENINGRAD
MID-70s TO EARLY 80s

THIS IS NOT a history of Russian rock music. If you need names, dates and chronology, you'll have to look somewhere else. This book is not about data. It's about love. Love and freedom. Or love of freedom... or freedom of love? Well, all of the above, I suppose.

Shall I start with the KGB search of my house in 1977, when my enlarger was taken together with all my supply of photo-paper? That would grab your attention, I think. I came home from visiting my husband in hospital, and the man who opened the door for me, instead of being my grandma, asked for my passport and showed me a search warrant signed by the KGB... and so on, and so on. I'll tell you about it later, otherwise it might give an unnecessarily gloomy shine to my story. My story is not about the KGB or persecutions – though they are involved – it's really about young people trying to have fun. The biggest fun of them all: Rock 'n' Roll. And everything that goes with it: sex, drugs, you name it.

If something stands in the way of young people who want to have fun then it's too bad for that something, whatever it is. Whether it's the tribal elders, or a rigid middle-class establishment, or Soviet Communist doctrine – they've got no chances. Young people will get what they want, that's how humankind progresses. No matter how much old people try not to let them do it. We scrambled out of the caves because of it, and keep scrambling up...

Everybody knows how and when rock 'n' roll started. It was on the African savannah where the first real humans invented drums, in the hot air full of blinding sun.

Out there on the savannah there was the first loud beat. And then another one, and another... And then it became a rhythm. Every cell in our body knows and loves this rhythm. It's the rhythm of our blood, it's the rhythm of life, it's the rhythm of our heart-beat. It's rock 'n' roll.

So I won't bother you with the description of how black slaves in the cotton fields of America sang their gospels and how this singing got to make Elvis, John Lennon, Kurt Cobain, Radiohead, Ice Cube etc, etc, etc. You know it better than me. I learned about Elvis much later than I knew about The Beatles – Soviet merchant sailors did go to Britain, carrying timber, furs, honey and caviar, but they never went to America. There was no trade between the USSR and the USA. There was Cold War between us, remember? That's why I first heard of Elvis at the beginning of the 80s, when he was long dead. I first saw him on TV when I was already here in London, which was in 1994.

This might help you to understand better what the Iron Curtain really meant. Not only that you knew nothing about the real us over there, but we knew nothing about you here. Or worse than nothing, for there were huge efforts made and no expense spared to convince us that you were imperialistic sharks dreaming of only one thing – how to destroy our beloved Motherland. We also knew that poor people in the West suffered horribly – rich people exploited them and there was no medical attention or education for those who couldn't pay. Generally everybody hated us because they envied our perfect way of life.

There was translated foreign literature, of course – Russians traditionally loved reading (there was not much else to do really, apart from drinking). But it was either about the hard life of working class people or farmers, or it was written in the last century. I remember the shock I had when I first read *Jaws*. That was something new! My friend's father was the conductor of an orchestra, and when they had a performance somewhere abroad he secretly brought back this book. The picture of a naked girl and a huge shark on the cover! The blue of the ocean! Soviets simply didn't have the technology to produce such a breathtakingly glossy blue. (They were too busy producing tanks and rockets, never mind that meanwhile we didn't have frying pans or sanitary towels for women's periods. Imagine that? A superpower indeed!) Again, I didn't see the movie until I came to England and bought it through the video club.

Anyway, for my generation in the late 60s it was The Beatles who penetrated through the Iron Barrier first. The divine harmony of their voices and melodies completely destroyed in a couple of years the image of the evil enemy from the West which had been carefully maintained for more than half a century by propaganda. It simply couldn't be. It didn't match. Somebody was lying here – and it was pretty obvious who it was.

The first song that appeared officially was 'Girl', and it was labelled a 'folk song' and appeared on a compilation of Polish, Bulgarian and Slovakian songs which was supposed to be pretty Western for us. But it already wasn't – we had our tape-recorders, and we knew how to use them.

Still, I was so happy about this that I chose 'Girl' as an accompaniment to my figure-skating graduation performance. Here I was, slowly dancing on ice in my beautiful short dress (I was 15), doing my pirouettes and jumps (not very high, I must admit, that's why I'm not an Olympic champion), and it was John's voice over the stadium! Or maybe it was Paul's? I never knew and couldn't care less. Gosh, that felt sweet! I bet it was the first public broadcast of The Beatles in my country. It was 1969. A year earlier Soviet tanks had rolled into the streets and squares of Prague, trying to persuade Czechoslovakia to behave. My mother said it was the start of World War Three – but the world either didn't care enough, or was simply too frightened of the huge iron fist. WW3 didn't happen. Lucky, really.

I knew people who were bringing music from abroad on tapes where, at the start and the end of a tape, a Spanish or a French lesson was recorded, to fool the customs if they decided to check it, which they often did. In the middle, though, it was Sergeant Pepper.

Anyway, once the process started, nothing could stop it. The epidemic was spreading rapidly, first through the more educated part of the population: students, who had more chances for occasional foreign contact, and children of ballet dancers or ice skaters, who went abroad to win gold for the Motherland. "Do you like Rolling Stones?" was the first question you asked your neighbour at a party. If the answer was, "What's that?" there were no further questions. If it was, "No, not really, I much prefer Beatles," then we could talk. And, more importantly, become friends.

At first, the authorities in Leningrad didn't bother to do anything about it, the reason being they simply didn't know. It was just another student party, somebody with a guitar sitting on the floor in a corner. Only instead of Soviet war songs (which everybody knew from their childhood) or romantic songs about the beauties of life in the taiga or tundra, he was singing in English. For a while, in the late 60s and early 70s, nobody cared. The authorities only started to worry when crowds began to gather at the doors of very small and seemingly insignificant venues.

Here I want to make a point. We started to listen to this music not in order to fight Communism. We were living inside Communism, and we'd learned not to notice it, like in England people learn not to notice bad weather. We didn't particularly like it, and sometimes it could get pretty boring, like at a school Young Communist meeting, but mostly it could be (and was) happily ignored. Most of us had a more or less happy childhood, especially as Russian children – with practically no exceptions – spend their summer holidays in dachas with their aunts or grandmas. The shortages of everything were normal and we never knew any better, so we didn't suffer from that either. So the musicians took their first guitars and tried to repeat the sounds from the badly recorded tapes not in order to defeat the oppressive regime, but simply because they wanted to play rock 'n' roll. It seemed like really good fun.

It became a conflict only when the authorities noticed that something had gone terribly wrong, and tried to take action. Each concert (session, we called it) was advertised through word of mouth only; partly because it was meant to be a secret in order to avoid trouble, but partly because there were no other means available anyway. Everybody knew everybody or somebody who knew everybody else. It was still a relatively small circle compared to the general population of the Soviet Union as a whole, but it was growing with an amazing speed. Take the concerts held in celebration of the Beatles' birthdays, organised by the giant of a man Kolya Vasin and where all future Russian rock stars learnt to perform. He started these as private parties for his friends in the mid-70s, with live acoustic music (everybody only played songs by The Beatles, of course) and wine that people brought with them. But very quickly there were just too many friends to accommodate in his single room in a communal flat. So he needed to find a bigger place. One friend had a friend who worked in a small venue, and that's how it moved on. From one venue to another, with crowds of very unusual looking youngsters with long hair and earrings and jeans, and broken doors, and shattered windows – not because people were hooligans, but because everybody wanted to get there first. Scandal after scandal: police got the news first, KGB later.

By 1981 Leningrad Rock Club had opened, at the Theatre of Folk Creativity on Rubenshtein Street, No13. That was a step! This was a real official place! It was the first permanent venue for all the bands which had previously played at school parties and such. Nobody had money to buy a set of equipment, musicians were using homemade amplifiers and stuff, and Rock Club provided a real set, a real stage on which to perform. Led Zeppelin would have laughed at it, but there was no Led Zeppelin in Leningrad.

It turned out later that it was a KGB initiative. They wanted to get us all registered, with names and addresses, in order to keep the scene under control. Well, so what? No one could keep *this* under control. Whatever was the reason for Rock Club, it helped a lot. The bands who played there started touring to other cities, literally taking the news with them, spreading the word. On the radio it was still only patriotic songs, or an official Soviet 'estrada' – a mild and extremely stupid version of pop, or classics.

For a very short while things were in a sort of equilibrium. The musicians were very happy to perform finally on a real stage, and there was a buffet with drinks! By then they were singing in Russian. Out of necessity, lyrics were always a strong point in Russian rock – the sound was always so bad that if the lyrics were weak then the whole thing just wouldn't have any real effect on the public. Musicians couldn't communicate what they wanted through their instruments because of the bad sound, so the words were important. The words carried a message. The message was mostly political. When I say political, I don't mean the lyrics were actually anti-state – no one would have dared sing about that – it was just that they weren't pro-state; anything not happily enthusiastic was considered political. Nobody bothered to sing about love – for that there was estrada.

At Rock Club the lyrics had to be checked by a censor before every performance. Every song had to be actually written down and presented to a special person in the office. If found unsatisfactory, the words had to be changed. Some singers agreed to sing the corrected version, some didn't and stubbornly sang the words they wrote. After that they were always banned for six months. They didn't mind. If they couldn't play officially in Rock Club, they played unofficially elsewhere. And by censorship I don't mean swear words or a direct insult towards the regime. Nobody would dream about it at that time. I mean things like "drink a glass of port", for example. Alcoholism is a big problem in Russia but it was ignored by the state, officially it didn't exist. To sing about port was considered to be a reference to alcoholism, it just couldn't be done. In this case, the words had to be replaced by "drink a glass of sour milk". And another one, when the song was banned altogether from a performance because of the words "You're my woman, I'm your man, if you need a reason, this is the one". It was considered indecent.

This shows perfectly the attitudes of both sides and the root of the conflict between them. Musicians told the truth. It was not specifically designed to undermine the regime, it was simply the truth. The truth about our life as it was, with drinking being the main activity of the whole nation. The truth about relationships between parents and kids, which were horrible: parents lied and pretended to love Communism all their lives and the kids didn't want to pretend anymore. Just about anything – but the truth about it. And the Soviets couldn't stand the truth. The whole doctrine of Communism as a happy future for working people was based on lies and was carried on by lies. In reality, working people – the majority – worked, and the Communists – the minority– enjoyed the fruits of the workers' hard labour. They didn't wait for the future. And the higher their position was, the more they enjoyed. A lie was both the foundation of this convenient system and the method of its survival. An open word of truth said aloud was lethal, and it was contagious. They probably didn't think about it that way, but they felt it all right, instinctively.

The crowds got bigger and bigger. By the early 80s, every session was a scandal. More and more bands refused to follow the stupid standards and the thing was going rapidly out of control. The more they forbade, the more people wanted to do it.

But it was only when they started to write about it in the newspapers that it became a really mass cult, in the true meaning of the word 'mass'. Russia was (and still is) huge. Information travelled slowly. What people knew and liked then in Moscow and Leningrad was still unheard of in Siberia or Crimea or Kirov. But as soon as they started to publicly condemn rock in the media, teenagers all over the country immediately knew where to look for fun. There was nothing more attractive or desirable for a Soviet teenager than what was condemned in the press.

That's when Russian rock music became really popular. It became prestigious to know somebody whose sister slept with the drummer from Nautilus or bassist from Alisa. Admittedly, there were more and more of those. The sexual revolution had arrived. Soviet girls realised that it was stupid to keep your virginity until your wedding. It took it 15 years to travel from California and Woodstock, but consider the distance and the obstacles – it took the Renaissance 400 years to reach Russia from Italy. Better late than never.

And that's where the crucial point of no return was reached. Young people realised that there were many of them. In fact they were the majority. And they were together in this. It was not me with my buddy in my kitchen with a bottle of wine and you with your buddy in yours with a bottle of vodka, whispering, secretly hating Communism. Apparently, there were thousands and thousands of us, loathing the stupid thing together. And we weren't in the kitchen anymore, and we didn't need to whisper either.

When Kostya Kinchev sang from the stage to the ecstatic crowd down below his anthem 'We Are Together' for the first time, that was the end of Soviet Communism. Some people didn't know it yet, but they were in for a nasty surprise.

Well, I don't really want to write a lecture about Russian rock music. I want to skip the whole business and start showing you my photos. I think they can tell you more than I ever could. I am (or I was, rather) a photographer, not a writer. Also, there are these captions under every picture, they will make things easier to understand, I hope.

But there are a few stories, which I'd like to tell you. You could call them highlights, maybe. Or just something which got stuck in the memory. It's like doing a puzzle – one bit here, one bit there, until you've got the whole picture. Or as near to the whole picture as you can with the bits you have.

I'll try to make them as chronological as possible, but I can't promise that I succeed.

And the last thing: I'm not telling you all my stories. The reason being if I did, very few people would believe me.

STORY No 1
CARLOS SANTANA
JULY 4TH 1978

WAS IT A JOKE, a hoax, or a genuine mistake? We'll never know. There was an announcement on June 15th in the Leningrad newspaper, *Leningradskaya Pravda*, that Carlos Santana was going to play at the Palace Square on July 4th as part of some festival. The announcement was tiny, but it was noticed. Carlos Santana playing at the Palace Square in 1978 is roughly equivalent to a Martian ballet company performing at Piccadilly Circus next Saturday.

Everybody got extremely excited, but in a couple of days there was an apology in the paper; yes, it was a mistake made by a junior somebody in the absence of an editor who's been on holiday, and this junior has already been sacked. But my boyfriend and I decided to go to the Palace Square on the day of the non-existent event, just to have a look. And there we made a discovery – there were quite a few of us who had made the same decision.

In fact, the huge square was absolutely full of young people, all dressed up 'alternatively'. Very different from the usual crowd in the same square who gathered every November 7th or May 1st to celebrate the union of all workers and collective farmers.

It was great fun at the start. The atmosphere was happy and excited and it was a nice summer evening with people drinking beer, laughing and playing frisbee. After a few guys played a few songs from the big monument in the middle of the square, it was somehow collectively decided to march together towards the *Pravda* HQ, which was through the main street, Nevsky Prospect.

That was when the trouble began. By then the authorities were aware of what was happening, and they took the only course of action they knew – they had to stop this unexpected and unapproved activity. So the truck-mounted water cannons were summoned to the far end of the square. And suddenly they started to close in on the unsuspecting crowd. I was standing right in the centre, beside the monument, so I started to take pictures of these trucks firing jets of cold water under pressure at boys and girls, who were running towards the river. That was beautiful! With a golden sunset as a background it made such a perfect scene! And so thrilling! I didn't enjoy the view for long, though.

Somebody suddenly seized me from behind, and a uniformed policeman with a bright red face and smelling of stale vodka tore the camera from my neck, chucked it on the pavement, and stamped his huge dirty boots on it several times. I didn't have time to say a word. Two of them grabbed me by the hair, with my hands behind my back, and dragged me to the police car which was already full of people with long hair.

They took us to the police station in the centre of the city, where we were all kept together in a big room. There was a piano there – it was apparently the biggest room in the building and used for party meetings and such. I can't say that our mood was miserable because it was still fun, getting to know each other, talking about things and widening everybody's horizons. Somebody started to play on the piano and it was really nice, until a policeman came in and ordered us to shut up.

At about five o'clock in the morning I was finally invited for questioning. Mind you, I had a two-year-old daughter left at home with my grandmother, who expected me to be back by midnight at the latest. So by 5am I wasn't exactly in the mood. They told me that, on the basis that I was wearing a T-shirt with no bra, they were going to charge me with being a prostitute. Well, I didn't wear a bra. Hippie girls don't, do they? But it didn't make me a prostitute yet! It was quite unpleasant, though. How can a woman prove that she's not a prostitute? And the stupidest thing was that they seemed to be serious about it. Obviously, they didn't catch me with a client, but they said that since the crowd was running from the water they couldn't be sure. Oh, I don't know... they were mostly drunk anyway, and I was really tired and nervous by then, so I was very happy when they let me out.

In the morning they let us all go. There were no charges as far as I know.

There were several consequences of this story. First, 'we' discovered that 'we' existed, and there were quite a few of 'us'. Secondly, it was the first time in Soviet history that an unofficial demonstration had taken place, and although it was not intended as political it inevitably appeared to be. And thirdly, it was described later in some Western papers (how did they learn about it? Search me, but they did) and that made us pretty proud of ourselves: we got mentioned in the world's media.

STORY No 2
KGB SEARCH
NOVEMBER 1977

I CAME HOME one evening after visiting my husband in hospital. And instead of my babushka (grandma) it was a man who opened my door for me, asking *me* who *I* was! I told him my name, and he asked for my passport to prove it. Well, I didn't carry my passport with me in order to get home. I asked him who *he* was, and he happily showed me a piece of paper. At the top there were thick black words: Committee of State Security – KGB. Dreaded words, even in 1977. Bad memories die slowly, and though they were not Stalin's murderers, the KGB were not particularly liked, to put it very very mildly. And with good reason too.

Now I realised who those two long, black cars I saw parked near the house belonged to. On my way upstairs I had wondered briefly who might be the unlucky one. Anyway, I came in. There were six people in our flat, five men and a woman. I wanted to change my clothes – I always did at home because I had a small daughter and I didn't want to bring the street germs in to her. So a woman KGB officer went with me to the bathroom, and was actually staring at me while I undressed and then dressed again.

Then I went to the kitchen, where they were all sitting around the table. By this time they had finished the search and now they were writing down the results. My grandma said they'd spent five hours digging everywhere: under my daughter's mattress, in a laundry basket, through the junk on the balcony. All my slides and negatives were looked at. By then I already had hundreds. I had a box of slides that my husband had taken of me, naked. They looked at every one of them, the bastards.

After the initial shock I asked them about the reason for their interest. I knew I hadn't done anything seriously wrong to attract their attention (not yet, anyway), but you never know. So they told me their story.

November 7th was the day when sovki (that part of the Soviet population devoted to the ideals of Communism) celebrated the anniversary of the Great October Socialist Revolution. There was a military parade and a demonstration of happy workers with red banners on the Palace Square. If you agreed to carry the banner for your factory or union, you would get a bottle of vodka afterwards, to warm you up after hours of frozen slow motion, sometimes in the snow or freezing rain. So, on November 7th that year somebody threw leaflets from the city's main shopping gallery, Gostiny Dvor on Nevsky Prospect, straight out onto the passing crowd. The leaflets said "Freedom of speech! Freedom of public gathering! Freedom of the press!" The leaflets were printed on photographic paper by actual photo processing.

They had caught somebody, then another somebody, and then somebody else and somewhere along the way they had found my address in somebody's phone book. That's why they were here tonight.

Well, it was a relief. I had nothing to do with all this. Never saw those leaflets, never heard about them. Generally I was far too busy enjoying my life and music to be bothered with any political bullshit at that time.

They all looked very serious. My poor babushka – who lived through two revolutions, two world wars, Stalin's terror, numerous persecutions of Jews, who lost two husbands and a son and now was hoping to finally find an easy retirement – looked very upset. I could see she was really worried for me. But somehow I wasn't. I'm not trying to look brave here, believe me. It's just by 1977 the whole thing about the state trying to control people's lives was becoming more and more silly. How can you control what music I listen to at home, and what I think when I'm drunk? And how can you respect somebody who seriously thinks that that is important, and makes it their job?

They took my enlarger to check it out, and all my photo paper. They also took some hand-printed books (we called them *samizdat*, self-publishing, manuscripts that people typed out themselves and then gave to trusted friends) and a box of pellets which my husband brought home from work. We never had a gun, it was simply that everybody brought things home from work; it was traditional. The salary was symbolic, and barter was natural, because it was the only way to survive. I give you nails from my factory, and a hammer, you give me a towel from yours, or an apron.

And then they showed me the one item which was obviously pick of the day. It was a mock Communist Party membership card in my name. And I mean mock, not false. It was a present from my husband and his friend for Women's Day. It was a very good joke, since they both knew my attitude. There I was, with a horrible grin on my face, and the membership number on it was 000001. And there was a verse, written across the pretty drawing of a mimosa:

Long live science,
Long live progress,
And wise politica
Of the Central Committee!

In Russian it rhymes nicely. Instead of a seal there was an imprint of my husband's thumb over my grinning face.

The KGB people were stunned: "Do you know that membership No 000001 belonged to Vladimir Ilyich Lenin? Do you know that his actual membership card is now at the Moscow Museum of Revolution?"
No, I didn't.
"Do you know that membership No 000002 belongs to Leonid Ilyich Brezhnev?"

No, again I didn't.

"Is it a serious verse or is it a joke?"

Well, what do you think? I mean, look at my face on that photo guys.

At this point the doorbell rang. It was quite late, about half past ten. It was our friend and tenant, guitarist Yura Ilchenko. (By then he was already my lover, I believe. I had just separated from my husband, that's why he was in the hospital – he took it really badly and had developed a perforated lung, which feels like a heart attack.) To his great surprise, Ilchenko was met at the door by an official looking man wearing a suit, asking him to show his passport, which he failed to produce. They let him in anyway, and after introducing themselves – you should have seen his face! – they asked him what was in his bag. Ilchenko had a really huge bag with him. He was a very practical guy, always full of exceptionally effective business ideas, most of them illegal unfortunately – the rigid system just couldn't accommodate his ambitions. So he opened the bag on our kitchen floor, and wow!

The great Russian writer Nikolay Gogol wrote in the 19th century a play, *Revisor*. At the end of the play there is a scene where all the actors are suddenly stunned by horrible and irreparable news, so they stay frozen for a very long time – no sound, no movement – and then the curtain slowly drops. I think Gogol would be proud to have seen the group of people in my kitchen that evening when Ilchenko opened his bag. The effect was gigantic: the bag was full of American jeans! Twenty pairs, at least. It was a fortune, and absolute contraband. Taboo. But I must admit, they didn't ask him where or how he got them, and they didn't take his bag with them.

But they did take a couple of American dollars that they had found in my 'treasure box', and the blessed Communist Party membership card, the loss of which I regret deeply to this day.

A few days later I was invited to the KGB headquarters for interrogation. I was thrilled! But there was nothing dramatic there, just a room with a table and a few chairs. My chair was in the middle. No bright lights into my eyes, no needles under my nails. They even allowed me to smoke.

Among other questions they asked about those two dollars, and they seemed to be really interested. Where did I get them? Do I have more? Who gave them to me? For what? Gosh. Both dollars were just souvenirs, given by friends from America.

Yes, by then I already had friends from America, incredible as it sounded. It was a young couple, John and Mary, travelling in their Volkswagen through Russia. One of my friends introduced us, and they were so impressed by my cooking – fresh vegetables, all natural, simple stuff – that they just wanted to leave me something. And the dollar bill was the only thing they had that evening. They actually wrote on it some nice words, "To Natasha with love," or similar.

The second dollar I got from another American, Bill, who spent a nice evening with us drinking vodka and listening to music. When I gave him a Russian classical LP as a souvenir, he gave me a dollar; again, not as payment, but as a token of friendship (we were really good friends by then – vodka helped). There was no way to exchange it for roubles as even the Black Market didn't exist then.

Then they asked me who had introduced me to the Americans. I could have said I'd met them near the hotel, or in the park, or whatever. But I was young and stupid, and believed all that official Soviet bullshit about how they wanted friendship between nations, and how they wanted peace but the Americans wanted war. The Americans turned out not to be the monsters as expected but really nice and friendly people, who were willing to share their money since it was the only thing they had to offer. Wasn't it great? But apparently, the KGB officers didn't share my enthusiasm. They wanted to know who introduced us. I didn't think it was a big deal, the important thing was that we didn't need to be afraid of Americans, they're OK, wasn't it what everybody wanted? So I told them about the friend who introduced me to the Americans.

At the time that friend, Volodya Kozlov, was serving in the Soviet army and had an easy life working in a photocopying department. Later I learned that he was immediately relegated to the laundry and spent the rest of his service washing soldiers' underpants. It took him many years to forgive me. I don't blame him, I should have known better. I've learnt.

My enlarger and photo-paper were returned. The books, the pellets and the dollars – never. The text on the leaflets about freedom of speech turned out to be a quote from the official Soviet Constitution. The friend in whose address book I was found was released after four months in the KGB's cellars, with no charges. The officer who interrogated him is now one of President Putin's aids.

I got noticed.

AN ALTERNATIVE BEGINNING
TO THIS BOOK

A FRIEND SUGGESTED an idea for starting my book, and although I've started it differently, I'd like to have a second go.

Imagine: it's the mid-80s, I'm standing under a cold shower in a very shabby bathtub in our communal flat in Leningrad, the walls are peeling, it's February, I have my eyes closed. I'm listening to the water. I'm receiving information about where the biggest Russian rock star Boris Grebenshchikov and his band Aquarium will play tonight. I need this information in order to get there with my photos and sell them, one photo: three roubles, two photos: five roubles. This information is a survival matter for me and my child. Money tonight: food tomorrow. No money tonight: no food not only tomorrow but for another week or more.

So, after a couple of minutes I know where to go. I get out of the bathroom, get dried, get dressed, get make-up, get my camera, my flash, my films, and my photos for sale.

My photos usually went like hot pies. I was not the only photographer involved with rock music, but I was the only one who dared to sell photos in public. Unfortunately, I got busted most of the time. In a place where you needed written state permission to fart in your own kitchen it was an outrageous example of a private enterprise – which was the root of capitalism! And on a more basic level, local cops in different venues just couldn't stand watching me literally stuffing my pockets with money when they had to live on their miserable salaries. Poor bastards probably thought that I was rich. I wasn't. None of my friends were. But most of them at least had enough food. They either lived with their parents, or had husbands who worked in normal Soviet places.

That was at the end of the 20th century, when in the Soviet Union they still didn't have any magazines about rock music for me to publish my photos. Sad, really.

Back to my shower. Some of you will see it as it is. Some of you will see just me standing under the cold shower with my eyes closed, in this ragged shabby bathroom in our communal flat in Leningrad. Which is just as well.

HOW I CONQUERED THE KREMLIN
JANUARY 1992

I WANT TO TELL YOU the story of how I conquered the Kremlin. It's one of my favourite stories.

There was a rock concert in the Kremlin, in the very Palace of Congress, where the Communist party always held its congresses (including the historical 20th when Nikita Khruschev denounced Stalin and his politics and declared an amnesty for all 20 million of Stalin's prisoners and victims, dead and alive).

Bands were playing for two nights. I went to Moscow. As usual I caught an evening train and all night, instead of sleeping, I listened to Alisa with some teenagers in the next carriage, who were going to the same concert.

I don't remember what I did in Moscow all morning, but by late afternoon I was already inside a huge Kremlin yard. Beautiful architecture, although Tzar-Pushka and Tzar-Kolokol (a gigantic gun and bell in the Kremlin) didn't interest me much. I'd seen it before. What interested me was how on earth was I going to get into the Palace of Congress? The security was lethal. I never had tickets to any gig anyway – I was not a member of the audience and I didn't want to be treated as one. In Leningrad it worked because everybody knew me and the band's manager would give me a backstage pass. In Moscow it was different. And particularly in the Kremlin. Whatever spare passes managers had they gave to their girlfriends and buddies.

I walked around the enormous building in order to investigate the possibilities. Main entrance: 10 cops per square metre. No way. Back stage door: 15 cops per square metre and special security guards with faces made of grey stone.

There was one other door, a small side entrance. I didn't know what it was for, but it didn't look shut, and although I could see a few guards inside through the glass, it was not as bad as at other doors.

My strategy was simple: I obviously needed help. So I turned towards the Kremlin Cathedral – you know the one, with all those golden stars on dark blue domes – and asked Jesus to help me. I prayed with all my heart. My favourite band Alisa was playing tonight, and I had to see it happening. Alisa in the Kremlin meant the total and ultimate victory of rock 'n' roll in Russia. I had to be there.

And Jesus heard my prayer. When I turned around I saw a group of middle-aged women moving towards that door. They were all laughing and talking cheerfully and all wearing heavy shoobas (fur coats). It was a group of cleaning ladies, as I discovered as soon as I joined them. I was wearing a shooba myself, and a large fur hat. We all passed through the door, waving hands to the guards, and proceeded further, still talking and laughing – me

too, though for the life of me I don't remember what I was talking about. I was probably just laughing inanely.

Then we got to the lift. There was a guard there too. One by one and in pairs the cleaners were leaving on different floors. Since I knew nothing about anything inside, I randomly got out of the lift on one of the floors and started walking purposefully – now completely alone – along the very long corridor which had numerous identical doors on both sides. There were two guards near the lift, and I felt them staring at my back. So I kept my head up and walked firmly. When the corridor almost ended and I had nowhere further to go, I knocked at the door to the right and guess what? It was Alisa's dressing room.

I asked: "Hi guys, can I stay here with you?"
They said, "OK, you're welcome".

Well, actually they said "nu davai," but that was it. I was in.

Alisa's leader Kostya Kinchev had great difficulty getting to the Palace that day. They didn't want to let him in and asked for his passport which he didn't have. It took a long time to sort it out. Obviously, it was deliberate. The authorities just hated him because he was the worst of all their enemies. They just wanted to spoil his mood before the performance.

They didn't succeed. It was the best Alisa gig ever. To say the crowd was ecstatic is to say nothing. In physical reality it was the strongest experience I ever had. There was enough energy in the Palace of Congress that evening to lift up a spaceship to Mars.

The next day Alisa's manager gave me an official Kremlin pass. An old uniformed officer who wrote my name on it made a spelling mistake. I didn't mind, I was just too happy to get it as it was. But he looked at me seriously and said: "You've conquered the walls of Kremlin, you deserve your name written properly." Wow!

HOW I SLEPT ON WINE BOXES
EARLY 90s

THIS IS A SAD STORY. I don't like it very much, but it shows a lot, I think. So I'm going to tell it anyway.

It is about my money. I started my career by making slides of my friends, the purpose of it being to then get together, have some drinks and smokes and watch a slide-show in my kitchen. Russians didn't have sitting rooms. Usually there was a bedroom, where people slept (sometimes several generations in one room), and a kitchen, where people did everything else.

Gradually the number of people watching my slides got bigger and bigger. The friends I'd been taking pictures of were becoming more and more popular. I had to meet the demand. Very soon I realised that it was time to switch to black and white photography, and I started printing photos in my room, organising a dark room behind a cupboard in the corner.

It was a time when rock concerts were still played in small venues. I started selling photos, and it was a success! I always had a queue, or more precisely a crowd around my table. I usually offered 10% of my sales to the band, and 10% to the organisers. Some of them took it, some of them didn't. Sometimes I was lucky and other times the police stopped me. They always had to let me go though because I didn't break any laws. No laws existed concerning selling the photos of the popular artists, because the phenomenon just emerged. Of course, there were movie stars and Soviet-style popular singers, and one could buy their photos as postcards anywhere, but there were no postcards of my rock stars. Few people knew the word then, rock star.

The venues were getting bigger and bigger, the bands started touring. I was touring with them: Moscow, Kiev, Archangelsk, Mogilev, Moscow, Kirov, Sverdlovsk, Mirny (Jakutia), Moscow, Tallinn, Riga, Vilnius, Samara, Volgograd, Kazan, Moscow... People wanted photos everywhere. The further I was from home, the easier it was to sell. With my Leningrad Rock Club membership card Number 013, somewhere in Samara or Mogilev I looked really official. Glorious days! Half of my profits went immediately to buy vodka from the gypsies or taxi drivers (no shops were open late, and then prohibition began) to celebrate the success with musicians, but I still managed to bring home more than the average Russian woman did. In Murmansk (up north, near the White Sea) with Aquarium I made 333 roubles in three days and this was after I'd paid my percentage to the organisers (Aquarium never took any money from me, to the very last day). That was when a standard salary was 120 roubles a month. So I felt quite proud of myself, as you can imagine.

The trouble was the concerts were irregular, and there was no schedule of any kind. If I got the news from somebody that Alisa was going to Moscow, then I'd go there too. If I didn't, I missed out. The whole business was developing so rapidly that the structures which were supposed to support it just couldn't catch up. Rock Club never had any information about forthcoming tours until the very last moment, literally the day before. Which was not so good because different bands required different photos. I couldn't sell a lot of Aquarium at Alisa's gig, could I? For you they might sound the same and look the same, both bands being Russian, but for us there they were as different as The Beatles and Rolling Stones for you in the 60s.

By the beginning of the 90s, rock bands in Leningrad were fully established as part of city life. There were more or less regular gigs everywhere, including the stadiums (we had two: SKK Stadium for 100,000 and Jubilee Stadium for 10,000). The sound was still bad, the amplifiers were still terrible, the light on stage was appalling but it was now available for everybody. Now everybody knew who Kostya Kinchev and Victor Tsoi were. And as capitalism was slowly creeping into everyday life, a lot of private kiosks opened near every underground station, selling goodies from the West, actually from Poland mostly: foreign cigarettes, foreign beer, cheap plastic shining jewellery, stationary, magazines and videos. That was where I decided to sell my photos. They happily agreed. So it was 50 photos at one kiosk, 50 photos at another one until I had five kiosks around the town. I would come once a week to collect the money and to give them a fresh supply. They generally took 30% for themselves, I believe, and trade was flourishing.

I finally started to feel some sort of security – it was real, steady income. I decided to get rid of my old sofa-bed which was totally destroyed after eight years of heavy use with my last boyfriend. I threw it away assuming that with this kiosk business very soon I'd be able to earn enough money to buy myself a decent bed. Didn't happen, though. Somebody knew better.

Since I was at every gig in town with my camera and my photos for sale, and had been for years, the police knew me very well. They had hated my guts since the early days. Finally they organised a resistance. They pulled some strings, and a new law appeared: "A ban on selling photographic reproductions in public places," signed by Lengorispolkom (Leningrad City Council). It was designed specifically to target me, and it did the trick. The kiosks no longer wanted my products – they were confiscated by the police if found. Now, any time I was arrested for selling photos, all the photos were confiscated and my money taken. A couple of times I had to spend a night in a cage together with drunks and prostitutes in order to stand trial in the morning. Once sitting on a bench I met my class-mate from 20 years before, Valera. He'd been busted for selling bananas on a street corner. So we stood trial together, in turn.

The funny side of it was that the confiscated photos were later sold near underground stations anyway. Cops knew better than to destroy easy money. They did the same with confiscated wine during Gorbachev's prohibition. They busted my neighbours for selling wine at night for triple the price (we had blue-nosed drunks ringing our doorbell on a regular basis any time between midnight and 4am for at least two years). Police busted the whole family. But they only put the man in jail. They left the woman at home since she had two small kids and it was a huge bother for the police to accommodate orphans. But the condition was that from now on this woman, Verka, would sell the wine the police confiscated at other places for them. So the trade happily continued. Now protected by the law enforcement itself, the blue-nosed drunks kept coming to our door. Most of them were peaceful and didn't want any trouble, they didn't know that the whole business was under special police protection.

But every now and again somebody would get too enthusiastic about something and started making noise. I didn't like it, for I didn't want my daughter to be woken up in the middle of the night. So I'd get up, get my dressing gown and go to the kitchen where the trade took place, and say a word. Mostly it was OK, not particularly pleasant, as you can imagine, but OK. But once, when I asked a company of three or four to behave themselves, a man replied that I'd better shut up, or he'd fill the bath with cold water, put me in there and make me suck his dick all night. This didn't seem attractive really, I have to admit. The bad news was that it would be silly to complain to the police, after all it was their enterprise, wasn't it?

The good news is that things like this help you learn to stand up for yourself. And it was small touches like this that strengthened my determination to leave that place for good. Motherland or not, I was starting to have enough of it.

Anyway, my financial position after the new law became catastrophic. That was when I started to starve. Before that it was still more or less fun. After this law fun was over. Now my photos were published in actual newspapers, which was great apart from one small thing – nobody bothered to pay. Or at most one out of 10 would, but the money was despicable, like three roubles 29 kopecks, when inflation was soaring and the official economy was rapidly catching up with the black market.

I'd send my daughter to one of her grandmothers where she would be safe and secure, and I would live for a week on porridge with no milk, butter or sugar. (Sugar at the best of times was a luxury in our household. Sugar on the table and a dozen eggs in the fridge indicated prosperity.) And herbal teas, of course, from what I collected during the summer. They really kept me going.

Admittedly, I was not the only one in a difficult financial position. The whole nation had just discovered that the low prices on everyday products all those years were artificially maintained. As soon as the Curtain dropped, the world market immediately started to affect Russians. The shelves became empty and everything disappeared. Retailers realised that it was silly to sell things for an old Soviet price – but you can't lift prices on practically everything overnight, not tenfold. First you have to make sure that people are willing to pay. And this was easily done: after a month with no bread people would be happy to pay twentyfold and would even say thank you.

That was at a time when a friend of mine said wisely: "If you must choose between a pack of tea and a piece of soap, you'd choose a piece of soap, of course". And indeed, soap was much more valuable than tea. After all, tea appeared in Russia relatively recently – some time in the 18th century – and people still knew of so many nice herbs to substitute tea. But soap! There was even a small but elegant poem about it, which is – in a very unpoetic translation – roughly:

I don't need Perestroika,
I don't need salami.
Just give me a piece of soap
I want to wash my knickers!

So I didn't buy a new bed. I slept on the floor for almost two years, rolling my matress to the wall during the day. It completely healed my backache which I'd got after sitting at my enlarger for hours and hours.

Then my friends came up with a brilliant idea: steal a few empty wine boxes from the shop yard, and make a bed! The empty boxes were not guarded because nobody sane would consider them valuable. They were made of a strong blue plastic, and six or eight of them would do perfectly, with a mattress and a blanket on top.

And that was what we did. We organised an expedition to our local liquor store, and from that night I had a bed. I covered it with a nice velvet cover, and you'd never guess it wasn't the real thing. And of course, the harder the surface you sleep on the healthier it is for your back.

Eventually my father, who had been telling me all these years that I'd be much better off working as a cleaner at his factory (I'd get a certain social position and a guaranteed state pension) brought me an old hotel bed which was supposed to have been discarded. He had huge connections because he worked as a transport manager for a big factory. He provided transport for a large area including buses, cranes, trucks and cars, both for the official needs of the community, and the not so official. Nothing criminal (he was not the type) just a bit of a personal touch. Grateful citizens and organisations paid back. Barter.

So, when I finally left for England in 1994, I left behind not eight wine boxes but an old, creaky single bed. I don't regret it, believe it or not.

LET ME START with a statement: never in my life have I been drunk enough to not remember how I disposed of a sanitary towel when I had my period. Ever. I might have been drunk enough not to remember the name of the guy I discovered next to me in the morning, but never in my life have I lost track of my ST.

Apart from once. And that was during the fifth or the sixth rock festival in Leningrad at the end of the 80s. The festival took place in the Leningrad Palace of Youth, a very uptight pro-regime institution originally, which gradually evolved to accommodate huge crowds of alternative-looking young people for rock concerts. It was the money, wasn't it? First, they didn't allow it. Then, when they finally did, they wanted the money to go to *their* pocket. The bands received practically nothing because of the insane state regulations restricting the right of an artist to get a percentage of the box office. With any rock event the management of any venue could be sure it woud be sold out.

And there was the question of security. The purpose of having security guards was not like it is here, which is to prevent people from damaging themselves and/or artists on the stage. The purpose was totally different: to prevent people from enjoying themselves; to prevent them from having fun. Ultimately to prevent the energy, which is the essence of a rock gig, being generated. Though obviously, they didn't think about energy, and wouldn't have believed it if somebody told them. They thought energy could only be generated by mechanical means.

And they had their ways. They wouldn't let people stand up and they would take away the first brave ones who did with their hands behind their backs (they would let them go of course, but later, after a long and stupid interrogation in the basement near the ladies' loo, making sure that they missed the music for the night). And God forbid, they wouldn't let people dance.

I had to walk around the stage in order to take photos, and if accidentally I moved my hips in time with the music, the audience appreciated it. So I was an obvious target. Every gig was a battle, with adrenalin pumping, with victims and victories. I had my war gear, specially designed by myself to intimidate the enemy. With all the shining plastic jewellery I could lay my hands on and my skirt as short as humanly possible – and officially no bra! – I made it quite difficult for guards to actually concentrate on their job, like writing a report about my arrest. They were distracted by my costume, or rather, certain lack of it, which slowed down considerably their thought process (pretty slow to start with, it was in the job description). Eventually they had to give up on me; there were no charges to press, and if a band leader allowed me to make photos of their performance, who were the guards to say no?

Anyway, by the time of this fifth or sixth festival I had earned myself the right to walk around the stage with my camera. Between the bands there was always a long break,

29

when everybody went outside to enjoy the lovely summer afternoon near the river. Two guys aproached me, dressed rather smartly, with questions about my photography. I was glad to talk to them, since I didn't know them (by then I knew quite a lot of people, particularly regular spectators, if not by name, then their faces were familiar).

But these two were obviously new, and they looked kind of official, like journalists from a provincial paper so I thought they might be potentially helpful. They seemed really interested, and they said they had a bottle of wine with them. We decided to go to the river bank and sit down and have a chat. So we did. As a lady, I was offered a drink first.

The last thing I remember was sitting on the grass near the river, laughing madly, with those two on either side of me. After that I have a vague memory of sitting on the back seat of a car, with those two on each side of me.

And the next thing I remember was waking up in my room, about one o'clock in the morning, with my head the size of Saint Isaak Cathedral, my tongue a piece of a sand paper, and no ST in my pants. Just nothing at all. And no recollection of what had happened to the one I had. And that was what gave me a shock. I must have taken it out and forgotten, but there was no way I could get so terribly drunk after a few sips of wine from that bottle. I had good practice, being with rock musicians for so long. I could out-drink almost anybody I knew. And I knew a lot.

I checked my handbag. In my handbag everything was wrong. Everything was still there, but everything was in the wrong place. That was how I knew that I'd been searched. And they were not journalists at all, but KGB officers on duty. I knew what they'd been after: foreign contacts. By then the situation with rock was scandalous. After Perestroika was declared more and more Western journalists were coming to Russia, where they quickly discovered the rock scene, still half illegal and still very much politically charged. Financially it was a complete nonsense: popular musicians were literally starving, their wives with children couldn't cope and some of them had already left by then. If they gave a gig for money somewhere out of town they could be busted and arrested.

Articles about the rock scene in Russia started to appear here and there. I remember an article in *The Observer*, with my photos which I had happily given to Sergei Kuryokhin for his foreign friends. We were all summoned for questioning for that – Boris Grebenshchikov, Tsoi, Titov, Kuryokhin, Vitya Sologub and me. They asked us how did the material get to the foreign press. Well, we didn't know, did we? Particularly I didn't know about my photos because they were everywhere: I was selling them, giving them to musicians, to my friends, to the friends of their friends… They could have been copied from my regular display in Rock Club, or stolen from my table, who knew? Then I said that since for Western journalists the situation was a gold mine – it was so evidently absurd – that until rock performances were made fully legal with an adequate payment, there would be articles everywhere. You couldn't keep a lid on this jar, it was too hot.

But I didn't keep the details of my foreign contacts in my address book. Why bother? I wasn't going to send them Christmas cards, was I?

I was feeling so bad that I took the next three days off my work. At the time I was working in the Leningrad State University photo lab, using state materials and equipment for printing black and white pictures of Boris and others in my spare time. It was very productive, but didn't last long unfortunately. We couldn't come to an agreement with the director of the lab, a former captain of the war-ship *Avrora*, the legendary *Avrora* that made the first and only shot on the Winter Palace which started the Great October Socialist Revolution. He was about 95 years old, and he didn't want to give me two weeks holiday in August, when I needed it to spend some time with my daughter during her school holidays. He wanted me to go in October. In August it was dead season at the University – no students, no tutors, no work in the lab. And no one to babysit my daughter either. So I left for good in August. That was my last attempt to have a proper job. After that I tried to work as a cleaner in the Naval Academy, cleaning an Admiral's Office once a week and all the toilets on two floors the rest of the time, but they cheated me on money so horribly that that was it.

But that wasn't the end of this story. A couple of weeks later I was sweeping the floor at home, with my TV on. It was a stupid programme, I don't remember what. There was a telephone number on the screen to call and make some comments on the subject. I stopped sweeping and suddenly found myself dialing this number. When I started talking I didn't recognise my own voice. I mean, I did, it was my voice when I'm slightly drunk and playing a nice girl with men around me.

After saying whatever I had to say I hung up and felt extremely stupid. I couldn't remember feeling so stupid in my entire life. Why on earth did I do that? Why did I turn the TV on? I never turn it on until I actually want to watch something specific, like a movie in the evening. And how come I dialed this number? I didn't have anything to say, and in any case I didn't care about the subject, whatever it was.

Then I remembered the last time I had used this cheerful girlish voice. It was with these two young men in smart clothes on the river bank with their bottle of wine.

That's how I knew that I'd been hypnotised for whatever purpose, and it made me feel absolutely sick. It still makes me feel sick to think about somebody violating my privacy by trying to enter my mind without my permission. And making me do something as stupid as this telephone call. The bastards. What kind of a state secret did they want to know? The names of my rock stars? Now every Russian child knows their names and so what?

STORY No 6
LUBERA
SEPTEMBER 1987

FIRST LET ME EXPLAIN what, or rather who, Lubera were. I don't know the details, because it never interested me enough to find out, but there was a kind of conflict between young people who lived in Moscow and young people who lived in small towns around Moscow. The fuel for the conflict was envy and poverty from one side and snobbery and arrogance from another. Obviously, Moscow being a capital city was (and still is) much better supplied with goods and was full of all kinds of material advantages, including prospects of a relatively bright future for the young. Muscovites were not particularly liked in Russia in general, but the close neighbourhood was especially jealous.

One of the most notorious gangs called themselves 'Lubera'. I don't know where the name came from. They had the most cruel and merciless attitude, and there were tales about their horrible fights and battles with Muscovites on the streets of Moscow, and basically with any strangers on the streets of their native town.

So, there was a big festival in Podolsk, a small town near Moscow. Why Podolsk? We'll probably never know. Somebody knew somebody from the city council, I guess. Anyway, the festival was supposed to be the first of its kind in terms of scale. Bands from all over USSR were invited, from Siberia, from Estonia, from Ukraine and of course from Leningrad and Moscow.

At the very last moment, when the musicians had already arrived and were accommodated in an empty student hostel in the woods, somebody upstairs got nervous. Or the news simply reached Moscow. In any case, city authorities said the event couldn't possibly take place. Never mind that the tickets to the local stadium were sold out. The bands were told to go home.

The musicians, however, having been busy drinking together for the last couple of days in order to get to know each other better – most of them had never met before – decided to ignore this. They simply said that they would play tonight as scheduled. And legally they were in the right, since the order to cancel the concert came through the telephone and wasn't printed and signed by anybody. By then state bureaucrats were terrified of dealing with rock music. Any decision they'd made so far to prevent it from happening was wrong and served – directly or indirectly – only to strengthen its position and popularity. So there wasn't any written document which Podolsk city authorities could produce. And oral orders weren't enough – rock musicians were not young boys unsure of themselves anymore. They already knew their power.

So the concert began. And it was great. For the first time people from all over this huge country were together in an open air stadium, with almost decent amplifiers. Wow!

There was only one minor thing that spoiled the pleasure for me. The police, who were plenty and who were surprisingly friendly – at least, they didn't arrest anybody who wanted to applaud standing up – didn't allow me to sell my photos inside the stadium. I spoke to the chief, I showed him the pictures, I explained everything, I even showed him a newspaper with my photo of Boris Grebenshchikov published – the first ever published. But he just couldn't bring himself to let such a thing happen in his presence. He violently rejected the idea of sharing my profits, which proved to me that in different circumstances the idea of a bribe was very much familiar to him. It was after all private enterprise – the very essence of capitalism. And we still lived in a socialist country, didn't we? Selling merchandise was not even a dream yet, it was still far in the future.

But I couldn't wait for the future. I went outside and organised a display on a bench near the venue. It was in a real wood which still surrounds Moscow as it did a thousand years ago, probably without bears or wolves, but with other local wildlife, as it turned out.

A large group of young people surrounded me, looking interested. I was pleased to show them my photos and talk to them, telling them stories about Rock Club and so on. They didn't actually buy any photos, to my disappointment – I was hoping to get some money for my train ticket back to Leningrad. (I didn't have a bank account or a credit card back then. Nobody did, or at least, nobody I knew.)

There was one guy in particular there, obviously a leader, with golden teeth and a heavy stick. He was sitting pretty close to me, but since I had my large bag with photo equipment and all my photos between us, I didn't mind that.

After a while they left. I got up to go to the concert – there weren't any potential buyers in view in the forest anyway – when suddenly I realised my bag had become much lighter. With a sinking heart I checked it – my camera was gone, the flash, and the wallet. I didn't have much in it, but still.

Well, that was it. I felt really really bad. My, in this stadium there were several thousand people desperate to buy a photo of Slava Butusov or Yura Shevchuk, and here was I, miserable and alone, robbed by the fucking Lubera, as I finally realised who they were. And it was all due to the police's stupidity and cowardice. The fat bastards, instead of upholding the law and protecting the citizens, created one criminal situation after another, and would they move their finger to find my camera? Oh no, although I'm sure they knew who the guy with the golden teeth was. I mean, I know they knew him because when I went there and told them what happened they said I had to be grateful and happy that I was so lucky: I didn't get beaten or raped.

Well... I didn't feel happy or lucky. I felt horrible. I didn't have money to go home. Obviously, I could have found money because everybody knew me, and I wouldn't just be left there in the woods forever. But it's not the same, is it? The point was to earn the money, not to beg. So I went to the forest to cry my misery out. I was sitting in the middle of a clearing on a tree stump with my nose running and all my make-up ruined, sobbing loudly, when another small group of young people approached me. About three or four of them. They looked older, in their thirties, which made a difference. Also, they were more or less well dressed. They were actually wearing jackets, not the formal ones, but jackets nevertheless. And somehow they all looked the same. Not exactly the same like twins, but very similar to each other, almost indistinguishable.

Since I was still crying they asked me why. I told them why. They agreed that it was pretty stupid of the police not to let me trade at the stadium. And then they offered to buy some photos! By then I had worked out they were from the KGB. I mean, you live, you learn, and it was obvious. I don't think they even bothered to hide the fact. I certainly wasn't bothered who they were as long as they'd buy enough pictures for me to get a ticket. They bought a few photos, for 20 roubles. And a ticket was 17.50, so I was OK.

Well, if you can call it OK. I had great ambitions for this festival. I had been preparing long in advance, printing hundreds of black and white pictures, knowing it would be the biggest rock event in the history of my poor country. I earnestly counted on finally getting reasonably rich. Instead I ended up selling five photos to the KGB officers on duty and lost my equipment. You never know.

But I was glad to find out that opinion on the matter was divided now. The KGB of course knew more about rock music – it was their job to get information – and they seemed to realise it was pointless trying to repress it, but the police still didn't.

And I have to admit, it was nice to feel the KGB was on my side for a change.

BY PURE TELEPATHY. I swear. There was no way to get the news otherwise. Her visit to Leningrad in 1987 not only wasn't advertised, but was deliberately kept a deep secret. Don't ask me why, I don't know.

I was sitting at home in the evening in the company of my beloved boyfriend and his buddy, stoned as a... well, whatever is an English expression for this sort of thing. Really heavily stoned is what I mean. Suddenly I felt a powerful impulse to dial Kolya Vasin's number, which I normally never did. We were acquainted, of course, but we were not friends yet. He was the great and famous promoter of Beatles' Birthdays, so it was a privilege to know his telephone number. I never abused it. But this time I felt an irresistible urge to call him. So I did. And guess what? His first words were, in mad shouting: "Natashka, Yoko's in town!" And then he repeated several times, seemingly unable to stop himself: "Yoko is here, Yoko is here, Yoko is in Leningrad!"

Well, I didn't waste any time, I started off immediately. Stoned as I was, I still got my camera and flash. I didn't know where to go, though. So I went to Kolya Vasin, to Nevsky Prospect, by taxi. He had already left. So I went to Boris Grebenshchikov, who lived nearby. They were still at home, and Luda, his wife, was worrying about what to wear. That was it. They were going to the Hotel Europe where there was a meeting arranged between Yoko Ono and distinguished members of the Leningrad Rock Club. I was not included apparently, but so what? I went with them.

At the entrance there were security guards, but not many. The Chairman of the Leningrad Rock Club didn't express any happiness at seeing me, but he knew better than trying to stop me. And that's how I saw Yoko Ono.

I don't know the reasons for her coming to see us, but for many years, until December 8th 1980, I was absolutely sure that one day I would speak to John Lennon. Probably I wasn't the only one dreaming about it, but it was one thing to dream about it in London, and a very different thing to dream about it in Leningrad. We even celebrated Christmas on December 25th, as John did, although the Russian Christmas comes two weeks later, on January 7th. We used to move a big lamp to the table, with his photo on it, and would put a glass of vodka and a piece of bread on it for him.

To see Yoko alive in this posh hotel was as surreal as to breathe under the water. But it was true, it was real, and we talked, and she gave us her tapes, and I made some pictures. Unfortunately, my flash worked only from the mains, and there was no plug in the room. I don't remember what we talked about, although I do remember there was an incredible, inlaid grand piano in the room.

When the meeting was over, she hugged me and said, "Bye-bye, sister". I thought I'd die. This woman actually hugged John Lennon, and now she was hugging me. So our wildest dreams were not so wild after all. Impossible was possible. Things were moving where we wanted them to move, despite the insane resistance of a threatened power-machine.

Thank you, Yoko! Thank you for appearing out of the blue as a truly magical sign that we were not mad, that there was another reality somewhere where people did what they wanted and it wasn't forbidden to love John Lennon.

PHOTOGRAPHS

38 SELF-PORTRAIT
St. Petersburg,
Summer 1994

This does reflect
my actual feelings
at the time.

SHIPS ON THE
NEVA RIVER
St. Petersburg, May 1993

This sad installation
decorated a view from
our window for more
than a year. There were
several of these ships
that had finished their
working life in such a
miserable way. Nobody
wanted to deal with
the junk.

In summer we had
picnics with our foreign
friends here. In the
background you can see
St Isaak Cathedral. The
location is pretty central,
like being near Big Ben
in London.

PROLETARY
Tashkent, Uzbekistan,
1984

Who's stronger?

This photo was made by
my boyfriend Bambino.

ELECTIONS
St. Petersburg, February 1980

The slogan on the left says "Long Live Soviet Democracy!"

All voters are heavily stoned, to avoid the emotional stress of having to choose one candidate from the one available.

During my exhibition I had a question: where did we get dope, being located so far from California? The answer is we were getting it from Asia. Don't forget, the Soviet Union included all the Asian countries like Uzbekistan, Turkmenistan, Kazakhstan. Also, later, when the Afghan war started, we started to get it from Afghanistan. Much better quality. Russian soldiers in Afghanistan, people from the far north who had never even heard about marijuana before the army, came back seriously addicted to smoking pot.

A PEASANT WITH HIS TOOL
Baltino, August 1993

A small village, three hours drive from the nearest town, Opochka, somewhere in the north-west. A truck comes twice a week with bread, sugar and vodka. Everything else they grow themselves. It feels and looks as if you have suddenly gone back to the 15th century. It is not preserved deliberately in order to attract tourists – it's just nothing has really happened to change it. Well, they do have electricity and radios, but no TV – it's too far from anything. They do remember WW2 though, and they say that Germans when they came for food were polite, unlike Russian partisans (guerrillas) who always took everything including the last chicken, leaving women with children to starve.

LONG LIVE SOVIET SCIENCE!
St. Petersburg, 7 November 1983

An iconic image of Soviet Power. Looks particularly impressive
if compared with the picture opposite, another iconic image.

IN THE PRORUB
St. Petersburg, February 1986

Petropavlovskaya Fortress. The name of this brave group of people is
Morjhi, Walruses. It's quite an entertainment every winter, and apparently
very good for your health. The water never gets colder than +4C, and
with an air temperature of -25C the water actually feels warm.

LABOUR LESSON
St. Petersburg, 1984

Future builders of Communism.

CATTLE
Village near Novgorod, September 1993

RUSSIA, MY MOTHERLAND
Baltino, August 1993

SUBBOTNIK
St. Petersburg, April 1984

How to explain the concept of *Subbotnik*? Once a year in April the
population was expected (required) to celebrate the Great Leader Lenin's
birthday in a very particular way. Everybody was supposed to come out
of their office and start cleaning up the environment. It always happened
on Saturday (*Subbota*). Nobody got paid, of course. Look at the face of
this woman, and her pose. Isn't she happy, contributing to the great cause?
Well…

BOYS CHOIR
St. Petersburg, May 1985

For the 40th anniversary of the Soviet people's victory in the Great Patriotic War.

HAPPY BIRTHDAY, RINGO!
Tarkhovka, near St. Petersburg, 7 July 1987

You can see here how negatives overlap more and more as
I was getting more and more drunk and couldn't be bothered
to rewind the thing properly (manually, of course).

But at least I managed to catch the atmosphere, I think.
Happy birthday, Ringo!

51

WOULD I LOOK LIKE
HIM WHEN I'M 64?
St. Petersburg, 1975

It was a big privilege to
have this book about
The Beatles. You couldn't
buy it in the shop, as you
might have guessed.

HAPPY BIRTHDAY,
GEORGE!
St. Petersburg,
February 1976

The leader of a
hippie movement,
Gena Zaitsev, presents
Aquarium
after their performance
(Boris is elsewhere).
Andrey Romanov, flute,
far right, died on stage,
aged 45, heart attack.

SERGEI KURYOKHIN
Rock Club, St. Petersburg, 1982

A very very famous avant-guard musician, composer, performer.
Founded Pop-Mecanica. Died age 43, heart cancer.

KOZLOV AND
SHORT SKIRTS
Near St. Petersburg, 1975

This is the guy who
suffered from the KGB's
persecutions by being
relegated to the laundry
while serving in the army,
remember I told you the
story about the KGB search
in my house? That's him,
Vova Kozlov.

THE CROWD
St. Petersburg, 1984

This is a historical photo. People were not allowed to stand up during the concerts, and if they did, police would immediately eject them.

A film producer, Dinara Asanova, was making a movie about the younger generation, and she needed a live concert for her plot. So she was filming *Strange Games* in a very modest establishment, and told the police not to interfere with the natural feelings of the crowd. And she had lights, which helped me as a photographer a lot!

ROCK!
Ekaterinburg, 1988

In the very heart of military industrial Russia, Ural metal workers
organised a national rock festival. This is a Siberian band, I've forgotten
the name.

Pure energy. Death to Communism.

YURA RULEV
At home, St. Petersburg, 1983

Marylin Manson basically sucks – this was done 20 years before him.
The band is Patriarchal Exhibition, heavy stuff (not difficult to guess).

MY BUDDIES (PERESTROIKA'S SOLDIERS)
St. Petersburg, 1989

In the Rock Club yard.

The one on the right died aged 26. It was suicide. His friend died of an
overdose, which he accidentally delivered, and he couldn't live with that.

GETTING TO THE
CONCERT
*Leningrad Rock Club,
St. Petersburg, 1984*

Before Perestroika, Rock
Club was the only place
where Russian rock was
officially performed.
Opened by the KGB in
1981, the small theatre
only had 500 seats.
It could not possibly
accommodate all those
who wanted to be there.

A window in the ladies'
loo was a perfect
solution. Ladies didn't
mind.

SITTING PUNK
St. Petersburg, 1992

The singer from a punk group I managed, Tokyo. This guy slashed at his arms with a razor during their first performance at Rock Club. I thought it was part of their stage act – the spurting blood matched beautifully the red and black set. But when I got to the dressing room after the show I found him sitting in the corner, pale and bleeding. So, being his manager, I had to take him to the hospital, in the middle of the night, where they stitched his veins.

HAPPY BIRTHDAY, JOHN!
St. Petersburg, 16 November 1986

The Zoo and its leader Mike Naumenko. Mike didn't manage to reach official stardom, although his band The Zoo was extremely popular and influential in the early 80s.

Died aged 37, an accident.

CARLOS SANTANA
Moscow, 1989

As surreal as many things at that time – out of the blue Santana was in
Moscow. The stadium was almost empty, because the organisers didn't bother
with advertising, but it was Santana alive and real, no question about it.
Too much vodka afterwards, though. It was always the case in Moscow.

PYOTR MAMONOV AND HIS FAMILY
Crimea, 1987

A good friend of Brian Eno, an absolute genius at the edge of being
violently crazy, Pyotr founded a band, Zvuki Mu, in Moscow which
quickly became a cult among intellectuals. Here we are having a break
during a big rock festival in Simferopol.

WAITING FOR THE CONCERT
St. Petersburg, April 1989

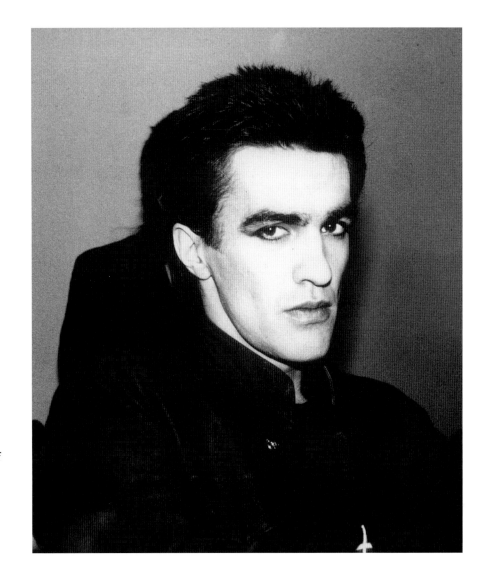

66

SLAVA BUTUSOV,
NAUTILUS POMPILIUS
*Lujhniki Stadium,
Moscow, 29 May 1988*

This is where his
stardom started. Girls
threw themselves out of
windows because of
him. Butusov was the
first to sing about
love and sex, not only
about politics.

KOLIBRI
St. Petersburg, March 1994

Russian idea of a girl band.

KOSTYA KINCHEV, LEADER OF ALISA
Rock Club, St. Petersburg, 1985

ALISA – UNDERGROUND
Near St. Petersburg, November 1986

It was not easy to get here – Kostya had trouble with the police, and
the location of the next concert was always a big secret.

The same week Aquarium played in the Jubilee Stadium for eight days.

ALISA ON STAGE
St. Petersburg, 21 November 1986

Red on Black and *We're Together!* – absolute anthems of the generation.

ALISA – WE'RE TOGETHER!
Rock Club, St. Petersburg, 21 November 1986.

Eternal suffering and misfortune came down on me because of this photo.
Cops, who arrested me for selling it, first got into a mental stupor and
then into a crimson rage when they saw it. Poor bastards felt a threat in
their guts. And right they were!

72 KOSTYA KINCHEV
St. Petersburg,
25 August 1985

Photo-session at
Kolya Vasin's house.

KOSTYA –
HEAVY METAL
*Lujhniki Stadium,
Moscow, 1991*

This is a real gift to the
photographer. By 1991
Kostya didn't allow
photographers into his
dressing room. So I was
privileged not only to
get in there, but to make
this shot.

WHERE TO GO?
St. Petersburg, summer 1994

After Alisa's gig in the Palace of Youth the company had to decide where to drink. The box, though it looks like it's part of the equipment, is in fact full of wine.

The name of the establishment in the background – Spezkomendatura – is untranslatable. Basically, it's a nest of local special police forces, not big fans of Alisa (to put it very mildly).

ALISA AT LUJHNIKI
Lujhniki Stadium, Moscow, 1992

On the left guitarist Igor Chumychkin. Died aged 28, suicide.

RUNNING IN THE GRASS
Dacha near St. Petersburg, 1983

BIRTHDAY PARTY
Dacha near St. Petersburg, 1982

Children start, adults will come later. In the background is a greenhouse
for tomatoes and cucumbers.

JUMP
St. Petersburg, 1975

At the old cemetery.
This is my first husband.
When the time came for
him to get a passport,
the police refused to
give him one until he
cut his hair short. He
refused to change his
haircut, they refused to
give him a passport, and
so on and so on...

That was at a time
when people with long
hair risked being caught
on the street by good
citizens and having
their hair cut with
scissors there and then.
And if they happened
to be wearing jeans,
then they would be
cut along the seam to
the knee as well.

MY BROTHER-IN-LAW
Dacha near
St. Petersburg, 1984

His name is Igor,
and he's actually a
photographer, not
the serial killer he
looks like.

It's hard to explain the
Russian concept of
'dacha'. Complete and
total freedom from
everything. No ideology,
no politics, no bosses, no
offices, no TV – therefore
no propaganda. The only
use for a newspaper is
either in the loo, or to
start a bonfire. It is just
forest and lakes, and
rivers and forest again,
for hundreds of
kilometres.

In the evening – sharing
bread, spring onions and
vodka with your friends
around a bonfire,
somebody with a guitar,
baked potatoes, then
swimming naked in the
cool, clear water under
the moon, a good honest
joint after that…
Freedom!

SILENCE
Iangenichi, September 1994

Every photographer has one chance in a lifetime to catch this moment
of absolute stillness. I thought about putting it vertically – to evoke
Freudian associations, but I like it as it is.

BEDS IN THE WOOD
Near St. Petersburg, May 1983

There is no explanation here. The reason for this surreal display will
remain unknown forever. Kindergarten moved house?

My daughter couldn't miss the opportunity.

PEASANT'S DAUGHTER
Baltino, August 1993

The girl is a student, she'll leave soon for her studies.
In the background is a winter supply of firewood for the
stove her parents use to cook.

TWO GIRLS AND A DOG
Iangenichi, August 1994

RUSSIAN SEX
Iangenichi, August 1994

In the wilderness near
Ladoga Lake. The famous
artist Dmitry Shagin
(founder of the influential
Mitki movement) and his
American friend are
trying to roll up their tent.

SAMOVAR
*Dacha near
St. Petersburg, July 1991*

Please don't think that
this is a normal Russian
way of drinking tea.
For us it was as exotic as
it looks now for you
(well, almost). It was rare
luck – we'd found a
real old samovar in the
dump, and had great
fun with it in the forest
near our lake.

WINTER ON DACHA
Dacha near St. Petersburg, 1979

My second husband and our dog Hudson.

This is 67 km from St. Petersburg, and despite the snow the train service is regular as a clock. It has to be, because in winter many people go to their dachas to enjoy tranquility and natural living.

OUR CHURCH
St. Petersburg, 1991

My daughter used to have her figure-skating lessons in this church.
Every Russian child had figure-skating lessons, not all of them
in churches, though. This church has now been given back to the
monastery to which it belonged.

88

MY FIRST HUSBAND
St. Petersburg, 1979

Near our new apartment
where we moved when
our daughter was born.

FATHERS
St. Petersburg, 1978

This is all my family. From left to right: my first husband, the father of my
daughter, we were already divorced by 1978; then our daughter; then my future
long-term boyfriend (the one who died at 32); and my husband at that time.
And our dog! All good friends, united by the shared attitude towards Communism,
music and drinking rather than divided by jealousy and hatred over a woman.

Mind you, in Russia we married at 18–19, and to change a partner meant
automatically to change a husband rather than a boyfriend.

90 OUR WINDOW
At home, St. Petersburg,
1985

Looking straight to
the River Neva, with all
the ships and boats.

MY DAUGHTER
At home, St. Petersburg,
1981

Trying my new nightie.

LET'S DRINK!
At home, St. Petersburg, 1983

My mother-in-law brought this lens from the military plant
where she worked. Everybody brought stuff home from their work,
even if the actual use in the household was doubtful.

I found this lens extremely useful, as you can see.

DANCE
At home, St. Petersburg, 1985

They dance not to celebrate Perestroika. In fact, they didn't even notice
that Perestroika had been declared. They'd been happily dancing like this
for the last 10 years.

MY SISTER
At home, St. Petersburg, 1975

Died aged 39, murdered.

No digital technology – just repeated exposure on the negative.

BORIS AND SEVA
My kitchen, St. Petersburg, 1975

For those who don't know, Boris Grebenshchikov is the biggest
Russian rock star and his band Aquarium is the most famous Russian
band, equivalent to The Beatles in terms of popularity and fame.

Seva Gakkel was his friend and spiritual colleague. In the first line-up
of Aquarium he played cello.

BORIS
Electronic Research Facility, St. Petersburg, 1985

98 BORIS AND LENIN
Mechanobr,
St. Petersburg,
February 1984

This photo was
considered politically
incorrect because
Boris is looking in the
opposite direction to the
leader of the world's
proletariat.
Well, bad luck for the
leader, I'd say.

BORIS – ROCK STAR
Leningrad Palace of Youth,
St. Petersburg,
14 March 1986

This is the first photo I got paid for! It was published in the first Russian newspaper about rock, *Rock Fuzz*.

The story of this newspaper is quite something. There is an island in the Finnish Bay near St. Petersburg, Kronshtadt, which has traditionally been a fortress defending the city from the sea. Normal people can't even get there – it's a restricted military zone. There was a man there who was editor of a local paper for marines. And he liked rock music. So he decided to moonlight as an editor of a newspaper about rock, parallel to his main job. He printed it himself, at nights. Imagine what he risked – with the Soviet obsession with censorship in general, and rock music being basically illegal.

When he came to me for this photo, he was wearing a shining naval officer's uniform, white silk scarf and gloves, and a dagger! He was the first man to pay me money for publishing a photo, nine roubles. Now he's the editor of a fat, glossy magazine *Rock Fuzz*. Glory to the victor!

AQUARIUM ON TV
State TV studio, St. Petersburg, 28 September 1986

After this appearance Boris was stopped at the exit by the guards, who
suddenly got concerned about his guitar. They wanted to confiscate it
with the excuse that it belonged to the studios. It was a long struggle,
but Boris won. As always.

BORIS AND HIS SECOND WIFE LUDA
St. Petersburg, 7 January 1988

Taken in the bathroom of their communal flat on Sofia Perovskaya Street.
In the top left you can see washed plastic bags are drying. They are
from fish, which they bought to feed the cat. Extremely environmentally
friendly, with hindsight.

BORIS ON THE HORSE
Solovki, June 1991

This was a huge event for the citizens of the Solovki Islands. They were once home to one of Stalin's most notorious Gulag labour-camps. Remote, isolated, terribly cold islands were a perfect location for untold atrocities, for murder and torture of thousands and thousands. Monasteries were closed, monks killed.

In the beginning of the 90s the monastery was reopened. Monks came back, and Boris decided to bring them as a gift one of the most important Russian icons, Mother of God from Kiev. Several other bands joined him on this tour.

We went to Solovki from Archangelsk all night on the ledokol, ice-breaker. It was June 22nd, summer solstice. The sun never even touched the water. Musicians and the crew made friends, and by morning had drunk not only all the vodka which was on board, but even the spirit from the gyrocompass (whatever that is).

AQUARIUM IN THE RUINS
Vilnius, 1986

BORIS AND MONK
St Petersburg, The Buddhist Temple, 1991

After 70 years of neglect and abuse (Communists organised
a slaughter house in the St. Petersburg Buddhist Temple –
of all things), Boris sponsored a few visits by Tibetan lamas.
It helped to start the process of revival.

BORIS WITH A PAPIROSA
St Petersberg, March 1985

Just to keep the historical record straight – it's not a joint.

BORIS IN LONDON
Oxford Street, 1995

Making a movie.

BORIS IN CHESTER
Chester, UK,
November 1996

In 1996 Boris had rented
a four-storey house for
him and his family in
Chester for the summer.
Summer extended to
November, somehow.

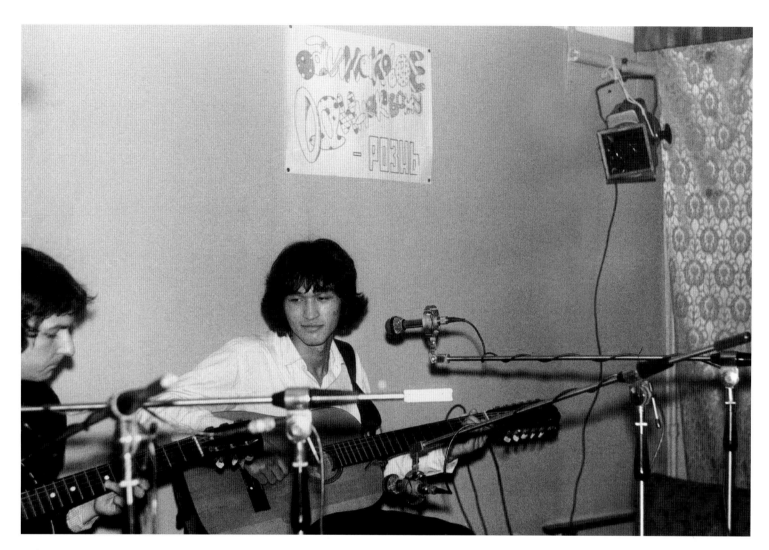

TSOI AND MIKE
St. Petersburg, October 1983

One of numerous underground sessions. Tsoi, young and innocent.
But look at him only two or three years later!

KINO – NEW ROMANTICS
At home, St. Petersburg, 19 February 1985

One of my first photo-sessions with Kino.

TSOI IN THE ARMCHAIR
At home, St. Petersburg, December 1985

Died aged 28, car crash.

VICTOR TSOI
*St. Petersburg,
7 March 1986*

There is no point trying to describe the meaning and popularity of Kino to foreigners. I'm not being chauvinistic, it's just impossible to explain how the most popular could be forbidden, how to be a rock star meant to be persecuted, how to play guitar was a political crime. It's too absurd to be fully understood.

Kino managed. Every Russian boy and girl knows them. These boys and girls are the only hope for a bright future. They will grow up, they will become adults, they will start to do business, or teaching, or engineering, or do everything else that people do. But it will be a generation that listened to Kino. Different. They will replace the poisonous foam that thrives in Russia now. Trust me, I've been there, I've seen it.

111

KASPARYAN'S WEDDING
St. Petersburg, 2 November 1987

Yura Kasparyan, Kino's guitarist, married an American girl, Joanna Stingray, the
daughter of a millionaire from LA. She came to St. Petersburg as a tourist, somehow
got introduced to Boris and others, got involved in the scene, and then decided to
produce an album of Russian bands in the USA. For that she needed a permanent visa,
and a marriage of convenience for the greater good with Yura (who was a very
handsome guy indeed) seemed a perfect solution.

And a greater good came – when the KGB learnt that there was an actual double-LP in
America they realised it wasn't clever to keep pretending we didn't have sex, drugs and
rock 'n' roll. We did, apparently. And *that* realisation opened the gate – the first Aquarium
album was released by Melodiya, the state-owned record company, the others soon followed.

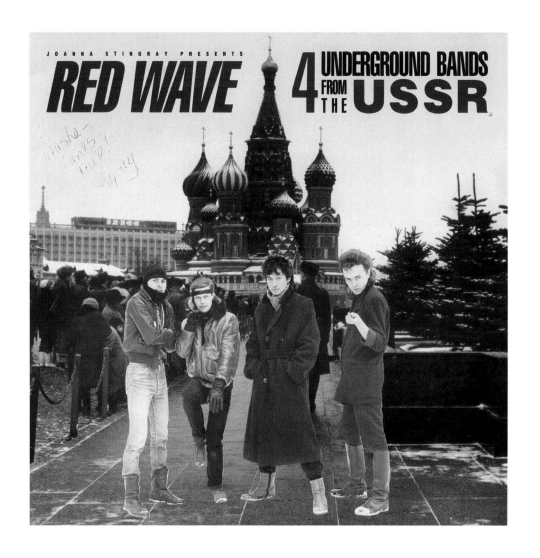

VICTOR TSOI AND HIS FAMILY
Tsoi's house, St. Petersburg, December 1985

With his wife Mariana and son Sasha.

TSOI AND KINCHEV
SKK Stadium, St. Petersburg, November 1988

This is one of the most politically incorrect photos I managed to
produce (there were a few). Not only were both characters at the top
of the police and KGB black list, but they're obviously drunk here.
And they have a bottle of wine opened! This is when Gorbachev declared
Prohibition, when vodka was restricted to one bottle a month per person
(it happily started the Russian Mafia, for the Black Market emerged
immediately – you can't stop Russians from drinking, it's ridiculous).

116 PUNK PYOTR
1992

Had a fantastic deep
bass voice. Died aged 29,
drug overdose.

A GUITARIST
1992

At one point I tried a new career as a manager of a punk group, Sudden Owl. Didn't last long, though – the musicians couldn't get their priorities straight, they thought drugs were the most important part of show biz (see the opposite page).

BALD 1
At home, St. Petersburg, March 1983

Just a friend. "The telephone is ringing, it is my mother on the phone!"
An involuntary illustration of The Police song.

CONVERSATION WITH THE SPIRIT OF THE GRASS
Dacha near St. Petersburg, August 1983

Quiet meditation in the evening, in silence.

BALD 2
St. Petersburg, 1989

Life is great!

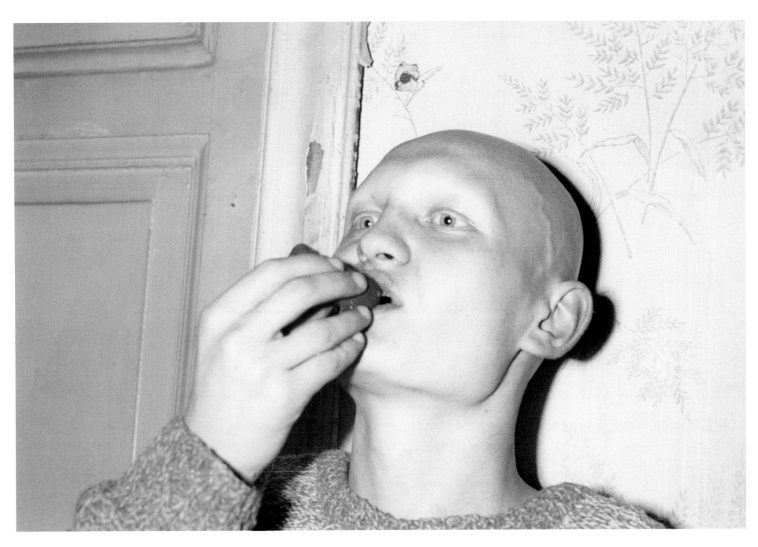

BALD 3 – EATING PEPPER
At home, St. Petersburg, 1986

MY BOYFRIEND
St. Petersburg, 1985

Died aged 32, alcohol overdose.

No digital technology involved – just a mirror.

A KITTEN
At home, St. Petersburg, 1979

This is the same kitchen where Boris Grebenshchikov played a few years before.

ROD STEWART
Wembley Stadium, London, 1995

This was my first encounter with a big rock event in the West.
One of the greatest shocks in my life – something that always felt
forbidden, illegal and suppressed in my society was suddenly
so obviously and gloriously approved, supported and welcomed by
everybody in this society. I actually cried when I saw it, with real tears.

WEMBLEY STADIUM
London, 1995

A magical symbol of a forbidden passion. Alive and real.

JANET JACKSON
Wembley Arena, London, 1995

I was invited to the after-show party. Imagine the thrill!

ROBERT PLANT
Wembley Arena, London, 1995.

I've got an excuse for this photo not being in focus – not only were my hands shaking when I saw him so close and he started to sing with this voice of his, but my bloody knees too. It made it absolutely impossible to keep the camera still.

RANCID
Camden, London, 1995

Nice guys from America.

RON WOOD
Wembley Stadium, London, July 1995

At one moment he actually winked at me. So I couldn't help it and
showed him my tongue, all of it. Instant contact. What would you do?

KEITH
Wembley Stadium, London, July 1995

MICK JAGGER
Wembley Stadium, London, July 1995

Did I mention that I was the first Russian photographer accredited to take
pictures of the Rolling Stones?

The excitement and general high was beyond description. It started with
a brief in a dressing room, where their manager told us, "Don't worry guys, the
Rolling Stones know about you, they will move for you in the first two songs".
There were 13 of us photographers, from Japan, from Brazil, you name it.

It was a highlight of my career. A turning point. After that I gradually lost
interest; Everest was conquered, if you see what I mean.

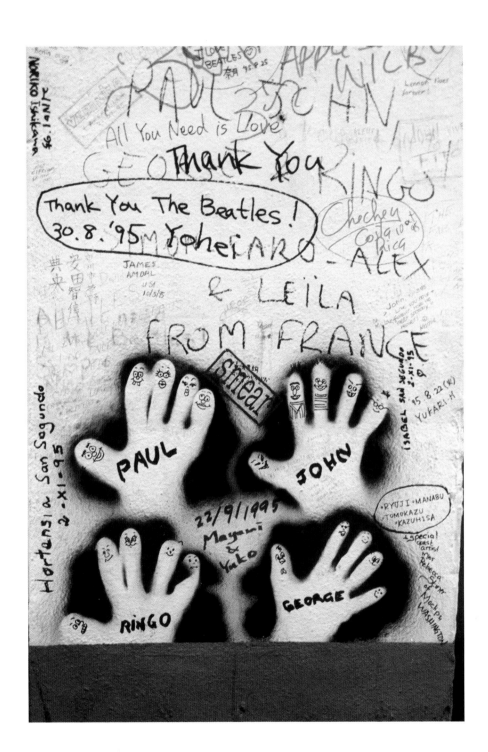

132 THE WALL
Abbey Road, London,
1995

GEORGE MARTIN AND NEIL ASPINALL
EMI Studios, Abbey Road, London, 1995

A press conference about The Beatles Anthology. I was the only one with a pen
and a notepad, everybody else had huge video cameras and microphones.

Still, we did shake hands afterwards.

DAMON ALBARN, BLUR
*Wembley Arena, London,
1995*

I've learned recently
that their song went
to Mars.

BON JOVI
Wembley Stadium, London, 1995

KOLYA VASIN IN PERSON
Near St. Petersburg, September 2003

This is the only recent photo in this book. Strawberry Fields, Russian style.

Kolya Vasin is now Chairman of the Committee for Construction of the Temple of Love, Peace and Music in the name of John Lennon. Basically, it will be a huge complex with a couple of concert halls, a recording studio with modern equipment, rehearsing facilities, restaurants, café, shops with merchandise, swimming pool, etc. The model of The Temple is already on a display in The Beatles Museum in Liverpool. Wish him good luck!

Part of the profits from this book (if there are any) will go to the construction of The Temple.

THINK GLOBALLY

JOIN US!

GET IT!

All You Need Is Love

DIG IT!

ACT LOCALLY

Committee
for Construction of

In the Name of John Lennon

the TEMPLE of LOVE, PEACE and MUSIC
in RUSSIA, Saint Petersburg.

DO IT!

Pushkinskaya 10, St.Petersburg
191040, Russia

tel.(812) 164 - 53 - 53

www.johntemple.h1.ru
kolyavasin@mail.ru

I HAVE A CONFESSION TO MAKE: I'm not a photographer anymore, I'm an aromatherapist now.

The link between the two is not really as obscure as it looks: I learned about massage in Russia when a friend of mine, a famous rock musician, needed help. But there is more to it than that – both photography and rock music deal with energy, and aromatherapy deals with energy as well. Energy which is generated and conducted by a living organism and can be directed to the audience of a stadium or to the client on a couch. So I personally don't see any contradiction here: I've done everything I ever wanted to do as a photographer, and now I'm doing aromatherapy, which is for me as exciting as my previous occupation was. One reason why it is so attractive to me – my editor pointed it out, I never thought about it this way – is that in this country it is almost beyond the margins of society's acceptance. I mean, not quite and it's rapidly getting better, but you know what I mean.

Compared to the position of a rock photographer a position of an aromatherapist here looks much less prestigious and respectable, don't you think? Money-wise particularly. But it doesn't make it less interesting. It is in fact very interesting indeed, starting with the astonishing results of my involuntary sociological research when I placed an ad in my local paper after finishing my course here. First, they asked me to produce a letter declaring that I was not going to perform sexual services. I signed the letter – who was I to argue with the paper? A foreigner. A newcomer. Then I started to get phone calls. I got about 80 phone calls in three days, all in the morning, all from men, and they all sounded very strange to me. Why only men, I wondered? Don't women in this country have back problems? (My ad said "Back problems. Deep tissue massage.") And they didn't seem to understand what it was I was offering to do. They all wanted an appointment straight away and seemed genuinely surprised that it's not possible. After a long and boring explanation of my basics – shoulder tension, stiff neck, lower back ache, general stress etc – one of them asked whether I would do a penis massage after that. And another one, after listening patiently through the whole list of health benefits of deep tissue massage, asked me: "Can we make love after that?"

On the evening of the second day of all this I realised that something was wrong. So when my husband brought the paper from the train and we discovered my ad between "Swedish Blondes" and "Mature Massage", the mystery was solved. No wonder I was getting so much attention – I was a new girl with a nice foreign name and exotic proposition! Anyway, my husband threatened to sue the paper, they placed my ad for the next week between carpenters and babysitters, and guess what? Nobody called. No one.

That's how I made my small scientific research, based on real statistics. The results didn't really inspire me. I was shocked. Not that young men are interested in sex, no big shock here, but the general attitude towards massage as a health technique was very strange to me. Very different from what it is in Russia. Now, having studied the subject and having worked as a practicing aromatherapist for a while, I think I know why: Russians never burned witches at the stake. This particular European fashion just didn't catch on. Russians knew how to kill an enemy, no question about it, and they usually hesitated as little as the next guy to do it. But they were never so afraid of women as to actually burn them. Maybe because Christianity came to Russia only in the 10th century, 500 years later than here, and it just didn't manage to root itself deep enough in the nation's mentality.

That's why the type of medicine you call 'alternative' or 'complementary' here – aromatherapy, massage, herbal cures – in Russia always was and still is a normal part of general medicine. In a pharmacy you'll find a list of up to 100 herbs and in Russian the word 'healer' is as legitimate as the word 'doctor'. They just have different functions: with pneumonia, a broken leg or appendicitis you go to a doctor; with everything else you go to a healer. Or at least, you try to heal it first, whatever it is, with natural methods, and if they don't work, then you go to a doctor for his pills.

It took Western women about 600–700 years to recover from that nightmare and to start emerging again with their precious knowledge based on countless millennia of experience and observation. The very knowledge which helped humans to become a dominant species on the planet before Boots the Chemist opened its doors.

Well, I can't blame them. If you saw your mother burnt at the stake, and your aunt, then you would find yourself another occupation rather than picking herbs and doing massages. Say, bakery or embroidery. Or doing the landlord's laundry. And no mother would ever allow her daughter to do it in these circumstances anyway; would you?

That's how the tradition of natural medicine that had been handed down from one woman to another was broken. First in this village and then in that, and then people just didn't remember anymore. The knowledge was lost. And the Church's universal concept of sin has included touching the naked body ever since. Until prostitutes, being politically correct, took the word 'massage' as their euphemism in the 20th century. And now the general population's opinion is that garlic and peppermint and honey are exotic and alternative. What's alternative about them? Aren't they basics?

And maybe the noticeable rise in popularity of so-called alternative methods is partly a result of a recent wave of immigrants from Eastern Europe? A girlfriend from Yugoslavia or Ukraine can do wonders, can't she?

So, if anybody asks you what the connection is between the late arrival of Christianity to Slavic lands and the total failure of the British NHS to cope, here it is. From my point of view the link is pretty straightforward. Obviously, other people might have – and indeed they do have – different points of view, but I still felt that I'd share mine with you. You never know.

INDEX

Figures in italics refer to illustrations

МИНИСТЕРСТВО КУЛЬТУРЫ СССР

Долгоиграющая

33

ОБОРОТА В МИНУТУ

АПРЕЛЕВСКИЙ ЗАВОД

ТУ—I кл.

Б

Д—2166

М. РАВЕЛЬ. ТРИО
ля минор
3 часть—Пассакалия
4 часть—Финал
Л. Н. ОБОРИН (ф-но)
Д. Ф. ОЙСТРАХ (скр.)
С. Н. КНУШЕВИЦКИЙ
(виолончель)

МИНИСТЕРСТВО КУЛЬТУРЫ СССР

СССР
АПРЕЛЕВСКИЙ ЗАВОД

ДОЛГОИГРАЮЩАЯ

МИНИСТЕРСТВО КУЛЬТУРЫ СССР

Долгоиграющая

33

ОБОРОТА В МИНУТУ

АПРЕЛЕВСКИЙ ЗАВОД

Б

Д-2165

ТУ—I кл.

М. РАВЕЛЬ. ТРИО
ля минор
I часть—Модерато
2 часть—Скерцо
Л. Н. ОБОРИН (ф-но)
Д. Ф. ОЙСТРАХ (скр.)
С. Н. КНУШЕВИЦКИЙ
(виолончель)

ПРАВИЛА ПОЛЬЗОВАНИЯ ДОЛГОИГРАЮЩЕЙ ПЛАСТИНКОЙ

1. Долгоиграющая пластинка отличается от обычной пластинки большей длительностью звучания (в три-четыре раза).

2. Долгоиграющая пластинка предназначена для проигрывания на электропроигрывателе легким звукоснимателем со специальной иглой (корундовой или равноценной).

3. Проигрывание долгоиграющей пластинки на граммофоне не допускается.

4. Каждую пластинку следует хранить в отдельном конверте, в вертикальном положении, перед проигрыванием протирать пластинку фланелью.

5. Скорость вращения диска устанавливать согласно надписи на этикетке пластинки (78 или 33 обор. в минуту).

6. Не запускать и не останавливать диск при опущенном на пластинку звукоснимателе.

7. Опускать на пластинку и поднимать с нее звукосниматель плавно, без толчка.